1. Introduction

For a two-week $300 payday advance loan, payday lenders typically charge in excess of $45, a cost so high that many believe the loan could not possibly be in the best interest of the borrower. Nevertheless, some estimates indicate that payday loan volume grew more than five-fold to almost $50 billion from the late 1990s to the mid 2000s (Stegman 2007). With the recent rise of the payday lending industry, questions abound about the characteristics and circumstances of payday loan borrowers, and the ultimate impact of such loans on their welfare. Interest in payday lending has grown among economists in particular because of the possibility that transactions in this market may reflect a market failure due to asymmetric information or borrowers' cognitive biases or limitations, or demonstrate divergence in behavior from traditional models (hyperbolic discounting, for example).

In 2007, Congress and the Department of Defense moved to ban payday lending to members of the military based on the view that such lending traps service members in a cycle of debt and threatens military readiness.[2] And in 2010, the Dodd-Frank Wall Street Reform and Consumer Protection Act established the Consumer Financial Protection Bureau (CFPB) to help regulate the market for consumer financial products, including the payday loan market. Historically, regulation of payday lending to the general population has often come at the state level, but the CFPB has authority to write and enforce new federal regulations to the extent that they judge payday loans to be "unfair, deceptive or abusive," and they have recently suggested that new consumer protections in the payday loan market may be forthcoming (CFPB 2013).

In this paper, I draw on nationally representative panel data comprised of individual credit records, as well as Census data on the location of payday loan shops at the ZIP code level, to test whether payday loans affect consumers' financial health. I use credit scores and score changes, as well as other credit record variables, as measures of financial health. Credit scores conveniently summarize one's credit history, and previous research suggests payday loan usage could affect credit scores. Importantly, use of and performance on payday loans does not directly affect traditional credit scores (such as the FICO score). Rather, payday loans can affect scores *indirectly* to the extent that such loans either improve or undermine consumers' ability to manage cash flow and meet their financial obligations in general.

---

[2] See "Limitations on Terms of Consumer Credit Extended to Service Members and Dependents: Final Rule," 72 *Federal Register* No. 169 (August 31, 2007), pp. 50580-50594 (http://www.gpo.gov/fdsys/pkg/FR-2007-08-31/pdf/07-4264.pdf).

In order to identify the effect of payday loans, I take advantage of geographic and temporal variation in access arising from differences in state lending laws. As of 2006, 11 states prohibited payday lending and by 2012 another six states and the District of Columbia outlawed such loans (see figure 1). In addition to standard identification strategies based on state law variation such as differences-in-differences, I also follow Melzer's (2011) novel strategy of exploiting within-state variation in access to payday loans due to differences in the proximity of ZIP codes in states that prohibit payday lending to states that allow payday lending. This strategy compares, for example, outcomes of North Carolinians who live in ZIP codes in the middle of the state – far from any payday-allowing state – to North Carolinians who live in ZIPs near the border with South Carolina and can access payday loans by driving across the border. The advantage of this strategy is that it is robust to state-by-year shocks and thus more likely to be immune to identification problems stemming from potentially endogenous state law changes.

This paper builds on Melzer's work not only by examining different (though related) outcomes, but also by employing a larger and, in some respects, more detailed dataset. It incorporates the entire U.S. over six years and subsequently more state law variation, and I am able to focus the analysis on individuals highly likely to have demand for payday loans by using results from Bhutta, Skiba and Tobacman (2012), which provides detailed credit record attributes for payday loan applicants just prior to application. Because only a narrow segment of the population uses payday loans, intention-to-treat estimates using a broad population sample will be significantly attenuated relative to the treatment-on-the-treated estimate of interest. The ability to focus on those most likely to have demand for payday loans helps mitigate a shortcoming of many datasets used in the literature – this paper included – that actual payday loan usage is not observed.

I also focus on consumers living in ZIP codes where payday lenders actually operate, or *would* operate were they not prohibited by state law. Using Census data, I estimate the relationship between payday lender concentration and economic and demographic characteristics across ZIP codes where payday lending is legal, and use the estimated coefficients to predict the ZIP codes in which payday lenders would do business for all ZIPs regardless of state law. This analysis suggests that payday lenders target highly populated, less affluent urban areas. Restricting attention to such ZIP codes helps ensure that individuals in the sample indeed have access when payday lending is legal.

Interestingly, the analysis of payday lender locations does *not* indicate that lenders target minority neighborhoods, conditional on economic characteristics of the population. This result is important in its own right because of fair lending concerns that payday lenders target minority neighborhoods without economic justification. Previous research on the determinants of payday lender location has generally been limited to analyses of one city or nationally at a more aggregated level such as the county (e.g. Prager 2009). Surprisingly, this is the first paper to use readily available Census ZIP code business data to analyze the socioeconomic factors correlated with payday lender concentration.

Finally, I also test whether access to payday loans interacts with shocks to the local economy. The period studied covers the Great Recession and thus large unemployment shocks at the county level are not uncommon in the data. This test has much in common with Morse (2011), who finds that access to payday loans substantially mitigates foreclosures after natural disasters.[3]

Overall, I find little to no effect of payday loans on consumers' financial health, which contrasts somewhat with recent research that finds both substantive positive and negative effects of access to payday loans on financial well-being. For example, Morse (2011) finds that access to payday loans lowers the likelihood of foreclosure after natural disasters by over 20 percent, and Morgan and Strain (2008) find that loss of access to payday loans results in increased bankruptcy filings. On the contrary, Skiba and Tobacman (2011) find that access doubles chapter 13 bankruptcy filings, and Melzer (2011) finds that access increases the incidence of having difficulty paying bills by 25 percent among lower-income households.

Thus, previous research suggests payday loans could affect credit scores, but the evidence is mixed.[4] The primary outcome variable studied in this paper – credit score – has the advantage of summarizing consumers' recent credit history and allowing detection of outcomes less severe than events such as bankruptcy and foreclosure, and helps extend the range of outcomes studied in the literature.[5]

---

[3] Carrell and Zinman (2013) find that payday loans have a more negative effect on military personnel performance in areas with higher unemployment, although this is

[4] As I discuss in Section 6, there are some plausible reasons for the differences in findings between various studies. See Caskey (2010) for an in-depth review of these papers.

[5] Some other outcomes studied not mentioned elsewhere in the text include the incidence of bounced checks (Morgan, Strain and Seblani 2012), job performance (Carrell and Zinman 2013), and employment (Zinman 2010). Bhutta, Skiba and Tobacman (2012) also study credit scores and similarly find that payday loans have no

The available data do not allow for a full welfare assessment of access to payday loans, but this analysis nevertheless helps inform the debate by testing for some of the potential costs and benefits of access to payday loans. The next section also discusses the payday borrowing process, the credit profile of people applying for payday loans, and state payday lending laws. Section 3 presents the empirical strategy for estimating how payday loans affect financial health. Section 4 focuses on the location of payday lenders and how state laws and neighborhood socioeconomic factors have influenced payday lender locations. Section 5 presents estimates of how payday loans affect financial well-being and Section 6 discusses these results further in the context of past research. Finally, Section 7 concludes.

2. Background
2.1. Payday Loans and Financial Health

A payday loan is a 1-4 week loan of less than $1,000 that costs about $15-$30 per $100 borrowed, an annualized percentage rate of 360%-780% for a two-week loan. Payday loans are usually provided by specialized finance companies that may also provide check cashing services, rather than more mainstream financial institutions such as federally-insured banks. To qualify for a payday loan, an applicant typically must show proof of residence, identification, employment and a valid checking account, and must have some minimum level of monthly earnings. If approved, applicants then provide the lender with a postdated check for the amount of the loan and fee (or provide authorization to debit their checking account). Finally, the application process does not involve a traditional credit check, and payday borrowing activity is not reported to the national credit bureaus Equifax, Experian and TransUnion. This means that payday borrowing is not a factor, like credit card borrowing, that directly affects one's credit score.[6] Instead, access to payday loans can only affect one's credit score indirectly depending on how such loans affect consumers' ability to meet their financial obligations in general.

On the one hand, usury laws that prohibit payday lending may inefficiently constrain credit access, and lifting such bans would expand financial choices and allow individuals and households to better manage their cash flow in the face of volatile income and expenses. Although the fees can add up to large amounts, especially when loans are renewed multiple

---

effect, but in contrast to this paper, they use a regression discontinuity research design comparing those just above and below the payday loan approval threshold.

[6] For an in-depth discussion of credit score modeling, see Board of Governors (2007).

times, these loans are often promoted by the payday loan industry as being meant for liquidity-constrained individuals with a short-term emergency need for cash; for example, to help pay for a necessary car repair or for out-of-pocket medical costs. In the absence of such credit, these short term emergencies could become more costly than the ultimate cost of the loan if, for instance, they lead to job loss or more severe medical problems.

On the other hand, potential payday loan customers may have behavioral biases or limitations in analytical ability that make a ban on payday lending welfare enhancing. For example, over-optimism about their ability to pay off the loan in 1-4 weeks may entice people to use payday loans, when in fact they are likely to renew the loan several times (which lenders are aware of), putting their financial well-being at risk. Indeed, administrative data on payday borrowers collected by Skiba and Tobacman (2008) indicate that many payday borrowers renew their loans several times, although it is not clear whether they expected, ex-ante, to renew so many times or not. Even if borrowers expect to renew the loan several times, Bertrand and Morse (2011) provide survey evidence that payday borrowers tend to get the math wrong. That is, survey respondents typically did not correctly add-up (and, more importantly, underestimated) the fees stemming from multiple renewals. Finally, by expanding credit at the margin, payday loans could exacerbate perpetual liquidity problems and chronic dissaving due to time-inconsistent preferences of hyperbolic discounters and again negatively affect lifetime utility.[7]

In this paper, I test whether access to payday loans affects credit scores. Credit scores are heavily influenced by consumers' payment history on their loans and lines of credit, and thus reflect their ability to manage their financial obligations. Scores could be positively related to access if payday loans provide an additional source of liquidity that can help people better manage temporary cash flow shocks and keep them from missing payments on important financial obligations.[8] Some previous research provides evidence that payday loans help mitigate the likelihood of major negative events such as foreclosure (Morse 2011) and bankruptcy (Morgan and Strain 2008); studying credit scores has the advantage of being able to detect more modest effects as well.

---

[7] See Laibson (1997) for more on hyperbolic discounting and the welfare effects of expanded credit access. Skiba and Tobacman (2008) examine payday borrowing behavior using data from a payday lender and conclude that borrowing and repayment patterns are most consistent with partially naïve quasi-hyperbolic discounting.

[8] That said, such a result does not necessarily imply that the benefits outweighed the cost of the loan.

Alternatively, previous research has also provided some evidence that payday loans may be financially destabilizing and therefore could negatively affect credit scores. A substantive negative relationship might reflect a market failure, perhaps related to the behavioral issues just discussed, suggesting the need for regulation. The primary goal in this paper is to build on previous research by quantifying the causal relationship between payday loans and credit scores. If a large negative effect were to be found, it would lend support to the concerns about payday loans.

2.2. The Credit Profile of Payday Loan Borrowers

A critical assumption in this paper is that payday loan borrowers actually have credit records and credit scores that could be influenced (indirectly) by payday loan use. Existing evidence shows that payday loan borrowers do indeed operate in the mainstream financial system, which is perhaps not too surprising given payday loan borrowers must be employed and have a checking account to qualify for the loan. For example, Elliehausen and Lawrence (2001) present survey evidence that payday borrowers also apply for and use traditional forms of credit (credit cards, car loans, etc.).

More recently, Bhutta, Skiba and Tobacman (2012; hereafter BST) provide administrative evidence on the credit histories of payday loan applicants, matching applicant data from a large payday lender to applicants' credit records from Equifax. The data allow for a precise match, and the matching results imply that essentially all payday loan borrowers have credit records, and well over 90 percent have a credit score. Additionally, about 87 percent have at least 1 open account at the time of applying for a payday loan, and the median debt balance across all applicants (including those without any accounts) is about $6,000, compared to about $9,000 for the general population. BST also find that about 60 percent of payday loan applicants have at least one credit card account (compared to 75 percent of the general population), but the cumulative credit limit across all card accounts is just $3,000 on average, compared to nearly $19,000 for the general population.[9]

Two other characteristics of payday loan applicants that stand out are that they are relatively young, and appear to be searching intensively for more traditional forms of credit. BST document that payday applicants had, on average, over 5 credit inquiries (a proxy for credit

---

[9] Note that the time period of the matched data in BST is the early 2000's.

applications at traditional lenders that report to Equifax) in the 12 months leading up to their application for a payday loan, compared to just one inquiry for the general population in the same 12 month period, and 3 inquiries for the general subprime population.

As noted earlier, I draw on this information from BST to form a restricted sample of consumers where the probability of using a payday loan, given access, is likely to be much higher than for the population at large. Restricting the sample will help provide a better sense of the potential size of the true effect of payday loans on financial well-being.

2.3. State Laws and Enforcement

Figure 1 describes how state payday lending laws evolved from 2006 through 2012, based on information from a variety of resources.[10] Over this period, there was a considerable amount of state legislative action with respect to payday loans. In 2006, 11 states explicitly or effectively banned payday lending, and by 2012 that number grew to 17, including the District of Columbia. The most recent bans were in Arizona, Colorado and Montana.[11]

Anecdotal evidence suggests that enforcement of state laws has been weak in some cases, and loopholes have existed in the past allowing payday lenders to circumnavigate state laws. In particular, the Consumer Federation of America (2001) discusses the "rent-a-bank" model in detail, where payday lenders team up with a commercial bank and use the bank's ability under federal law to charge a higher interest rate than state law allows. However, by 2006 federal banking regulators effectively ended this practice (Mann and Hawkins 2007), and state laws appear to be strictly enforced in recent years. Indeed, as I discuss in more detail in Section 4.2, figures 2 and 3 provide evidence from Census data that state laws bind. In addition, recent research by Avery and Samolyk (2011) using a 2009 data supplement to the Current Population Survey indicates that people in the states with outright or effective bans are highly unlikely to get payday loans. Importantly, their results also imply that the internet generally does not suffice as a mechanism to provide payday loans in states that restrict payday lending, which Pew (2012)

---

[10] Sources include a series of reports from the Consumer Federation of America, which can be accessed at http://www.paydayloaninfo.org/research-a-reports, The Pew Charitable Trusts (http://www.pewstates.org/research/data-visualizations/state-payday-loan-regulation-and-usage-rates-85899405695), the National Conference of State Legislatures (http://www.ncsl.org/issues-research/banking/payday-lending-state-statutes.aspx), Credit.com (http://www.credit.com/credit-law/payday-loan-laws/), and state government websites and local news articles about state legislative actions on payday lending.

[11] Colorado is considered to have effectively ban payday lending by stipulating a minimum loan term of six months, along with price caps, that prevent typical 2-4 week payday loans that have been scrutinized.

concludes as well in separate research. Consistent with those findings, the websites of the largest payday lending companies appear to prohibit applications from people residing in states that restrict such loans.

3. Empirical Strategy

3.1. Main Specifications

The primary goal of this paper is to estimate the effect of payday loans on financial well-being. To that end, I exploit within-state variation in access to payday loans arising from changes in state laws, as well as across-ZIP-code variation within payday-prohibiting states, as in Melzer (2011), in the following regression specification:

$$y_{izcst} = \alpha + \beta_1(PDaccess_{zt}) + \beta_2(PDaccess_{zt} \cdot unemp\,shock_{ct}) \\ + \beta_3(unemp\,shock_{ct}) + \beta_4(border_{zt}) + \beta_5(HPIgrowth_{ct}) + \mathbf{x}'_i\boldsymbol{\delta} + \gamma_s + \mu_t + \varepsilon_{izcst} \quad (1)$$

The dependent variable is a measure of financial well-being from the credit record data (discussed later) for individual i, in ZIP code z, county c, state s and year t. As discussed earlier, payday loan access (*PDaccess*) varies at the ZIP code level because in states where payday lending is banned, some ZIP codes in those states will still have access because of their close proximity to states that allow payday lending. Following Melzer (2011), I consider a ZIP code in a ban state to have access if it is less than 25 miles from a ZIP code in another state that allows payday lending.

I also interact payday loan access with county unemployment shocks, measured as the difference between the unemployment rate in year t and the average unemployment rate for the county from 2000 to 2006. Although someone who loses his job may not be able to get a payday loan because they no longer have a regular paycheck (although a regular unemployment check may suffice), a spouse or other member of the household may still be able to access payday loans. A household suffering from an income shock may turn to payday loans to help smooth consumption, expecting that the lost income will soon be replaced from a new job. However, borrowers may systematically overestimate the likelihood of replacing their income, and payday loans could then make a tough financial situation even worse. Alternatively, borrowers could use the proceeds of a payday loan to help make minimum payments on other financial obligations to avoid becoming delinquent on accounts that get reported to credit bureaus and feed into their credit score.

The specification also includes controls for whether a ZIP code borders another state; house price appreciation at the county level over the previous two years in order to help control for the extent of the housing bust; and a vector **x** of socioeconomic characteristics.[12] Finally, equation (1) includes state fixed effects and time fixed effects and thus, as noted earlier, the effect of access to payday loans will be identified from within-state variation.

There are three sources of within-state variation. First, residents of a given state can lose access to payday loans simply because their state implements a ban of such loans. Second, some residents of states with a ban still have access through a bordering state if they live close to the border, whereas other residents of the same state living in the interior do not have access. And third, those who have access through a border state can lose access when that bordering state implements a ban. For example, residents of Massachusetts who had access to payday loans through New Hampshire lost that access in 2009 when New Hampshire imposed a ban.

A benefit of the detailed data used in this paper is that state-by-year fixed effects, which control for state-year shocks that could be correlated with state law changes and outcomes, can be included:

$$y_{izcst} = \alpha + \beta_1(PDaccess_{zt}) + \beta_2(PDaccess_{zt} \cdot unemp\,shock_{ct}) \\ + \beta_3(unemp\,shock_{ct}) + \beta_4(border_{zt}) + \beta_5(HPIgrowth_{ct}) + \mathbf{x}'_i\boldsymbol{\delta} + \eta_{st} + \varepsilon_{izcst} \qquad (2)$$

Identification in this specification comes from the second and third sources of variation just discussed. Obviously, a key assumption is that people actually cross state borders to get payday loans. Anecdotal evidence suggests this occurs, and Melzer (2011) provides evidence that payday lenders open shops along borders with payday-prohibiting states, presumably because people will travel across the border to get payday loans. In Section 4.4, I provide similar evidence.

3.2. Regressions Using a Restricted Sample

---

[12] Although **x** has a subscript *i*, I am mostly limited to using census tract proxies for individual characteristics. Census tracts are considerably smaller geographic areas than ZIP codes and are designed to be relatively homogenous with respect to socio-economic characteristics.

As a starting point, equations (1) and (2) are estimated using an unrestricted sample representing all consumers in the U.S.. However, because only a narrow segment of the population typically uses payday loans, estimates of β_1 and β_2 will be substantially smaller than the treatment-on-the-treated estimates of the effect of payday loan borrowing that are ultimately of interest.[13] In other words, because borrowing on payday loans is not directly observed in the data, and because the probability of payday loan use is small, the reduced form estimates from equations (1) and (2) will be attenuated relative to the estimates of interest.

To address this issue, I also estimate equations (1) and (2) using a restricted sample of consumers where the probability of borrowing on payday loans given access is likely to be much higher. I restrict the sample along two dimensions. The first dimension relates to individual characteristics that have been shown in past research to be closely related to payday loan use, as discussed will be discussed in more detail in Section 5.1. The second dimension relates to where individuals live, and whether their residential ZIP code location is the type of area that actually attracts payday lenders – for example ZIP codes with a high enough concentration of people with potential demand for payday loans in order to operate profitably.[14]

3.3. Identifying "Payday ZIPs"

In order to identify ZIP codes that are attractive to payday lenders, I run a negative binomial regression of the count of payday stores in a given ZIP code, z, in 2008 on two scale variables (ZIP code population and ZIP code total number of establishments) and a variety of ZIP code socioeconomic characteristics:[15]

$$E(PDstores_z) = \exp\{\alpha_0 + \alpha_1 \ln(pop_z) + \alpha_2 \ln(estab_z) + \mathbf{x}'_z \boldsymbol{\beta}\} \qquad (3)$$

Equation (3) is estimated using only those ZIP codes in states that allowed payday lending throughout the 2006-2012 period, and then I generate predictions of the number of payday loan stores across ZIP codes in *all* states using the estimated coefficients (that is, both in-sample and

---

[13] For example, Avery and Samolyk (2011) find that less than 5 percent of households report having used payday loans at least once during 2008.

[14] This restriction may be less important for estimates of equation **Error! Reference source not found.** since they are identified from people who must travel to other to get payday loans anyway. On the other hand, payday lenders might only operate in places along the border if there are ZIP codes just across the border that would have attracted payday lenders had state law not prohibited them.

[15] Negative binomial regression is a more general version of Poisson regression that allows the variance to exceed the mean.

out-of-sample predictions). Finally, I construct expected payday stores per capita (*PDpercap*) for every ZIP code as:

$$\widehat{PDpercap}_z = \frac{\widehat{PDstores}_z}{population_z} \quad (4)$$

and define "payday ZIPs" as those ZIP codes with $\widehat{PDpercap}_z$ in the top one-third of ZIP codes.

4. Where Do Payday Lenders Operate? Evidence from Census Data

4.1. ZIP Code Socioeconomic and Payday Lender Location Data

I employ two primary sources of data to estimate equation (3) and obtain estimates of neighborhood payday store concentration. The first are Census ZIP Code Business Patterns (ZCBP) data, and the second are ZIP code socioeconomic characteristics from the 2000 Census. The ZCBP data have been published annually since 1994, and measure the number of establishments, number of employees and total payroll by ZIP and detailed industry code.[16] Two North American Industrial Classification System (NAICS) codes in particular capture payday lending establishments:

1) *Nondepository consumer lending* (522291): establishments primarily engaged in making unsecured cash loans to consumers
2) *Other activities related to credit intermediation* (522390): establishments primarily engaged in facilitating credit intermediation (except mortgage and loan brokerage; and financial transactions processing, reserve, and clearinghouse activities), including check cashing services and money order issuance services

In 2008, there were about 14,500 establishments in industry 522291 and just over 20,000 establishments in industry 522390 across the entire U.S. The total number of payday establishments based on the ZCBP may be on the high side (for instance, Stegman (2007) cites industry figures estimating a total of around 25,000 storefronts) because not all check-cashing outlets, especially those in states that prohibit payday lending, necessarily offer payday loans. Also, these six-digit NAICS industries can include other types of businesses besides payday lenders and check-cashers to the extent that they still fit within the industry definition.

---

[16] Note that these data exclude information on non-employer firms. For more information on the ZCBP data, see http://www.census.gov/econ/cbp/index.html.

Although the ZCBP data provide a noisy measure of payday lending stores in a given ZIP code, my interest lies in the geographic variation of stores rather than in their total number, and therefore the ZCBP should serve the analysis well. Indeed, state-level variation in the number of establishments per person follows expected patterns. For instance, several southern states (Mississippi, South Carolina and Louisiana) have the highest number of payday establishments per person, which is very similar to Prager's (2009) finding.

Table 1 provides summary statistics from the ZCBP and the 2000 Census data. The sample of ZIP codes includes only those in states that allowed payday lending throughout the 2006 to 2012 period (excluding Alaska and Hawaii); those in metropolitan areas; and those with at least one establishment employee, at least 1000 residents, and no more than 50 percent of the population residing in group quarters. These restrictions yield a sample of 8,666 ZIP codes, with an average population of just over 17,000.

On average, these ZIP codes contain about 400 establishments across all industries, and about 2.4 establishments in the payday lending industries. The median ZIP code, however, contains just one payday industry establishment. The other variables listed help describe the income, wealth and demographic characteristics of the ZIP codes, which may influence the demand for payday loans. Median family income ranges from about $32,000 at the 10th percentile to over $75,000 at the 90th percentile. Median home value and the homeownership rate also vary considerably across ZIP codes, as does educational attainment. Finally, as Caskey (2005) notes, previous survey research indicates that payday loan customers tend to be young and also tend to be female. I will therefore include the share of adults under the age of 40 and the single-mother share of families as additional predictors of the number of payday lending establishments.

4.2. Are Payday Lending Laws Binding?

The ZCBP data suggest that state payday lending restrictions have had bite in recent years. Figure 2 indicates that the state-level concentration of payday lending stores is considerably higher in states that permit payday lending, whereas the concentration of establishments in another nondepository consumer credit industry (522292 – real estate credit) is much more similar across the two groups of states. (As noted above, because the industry codes used to identify payday lenders include non-payday-lending establishments, the concentration of establishments in these industries is not expected to be zero in payday-prohibiting states.)

Figure 3 indicates that the concentration of payday lending stores declined by about 50 percent from 2006 through 2011 in the states that passed laws prohibiting payday lending during this period (black bars). In 2007, the concentration of payday lending stores in these states was almost double the concentration in states where payday lending was prohibited throughout the period. But by 2011, the concentrations in these two groups of states were nearly identical. To be sure, there was a slight down trend in concentration in states that allowed payday lending throughout the period, but this trend was not nearly as pronounced as for the states that implemented bans or significant restrictions.

4.3. Socioeconomic Determinants of Neighborhood Payday Lender Concentration

Table 2a displays negative binomial (similar to Poisson regression) estimates of equation (3). As noted in the introduction, these results are of interest in their own right because of concerns about predatory lending and the concentration of payday lenders in minority neighborhoods. With that in mind, I estimate two models, the first leaving out race and ethnic composition variables and the second including them. Each specification allows for a nonlinear relationship between the number of payday industry establishments and median family income, and includes state fixed effects. Standard errors are clustered at the state level.

The second column of table 2a shows that one of the three race/ethnicity variables is statistically significant, and the likelihood ratio test statistic rejects the hypothesis that all three minority coefficients are zero. But as table 2b shows, the magnitudes of these coefficients are quite small. For example, a one standard deviation increase in the Black population share (an increase of 18 percentage points) would increase the number of payday stores by just 2 percent, all else equal. In contrast, home values, educational attainment and median family income are strongly related to the number of payday stores. Payroll per worker (the wages of local employees, not necessarily residents of the ZIP code) also appears to have a strong relationship with the number of payday lenders. Interestingly, a rise in median family income from $40,000 to $60,000 appears to have a *positive* effect on the number of payday establishments, but that effect is of course conditional on local wages, home values, educational attainment and the other variables in the model. These other income and wealth measures (including educational attainment) have strong negative effects on payday lender presence.

Finally, to identify high-concentration ZIP codes or "payday ZIPs", I generate predicted values and plug them into equation (4). To obtain the predicted values, I use a more concise regression model with only the scale, income and wealth variables (including educational attainment), and omit state fixed effects so that I can generate out-of-sample predictions for ZIP codes in states that prohibit payday lending.

Analysis of the in-sample predictions suggests that the model does a good job of predicting the number of ZIP code payday stores. The correlation between predicted and actual values is 0.73, and the distribution of the predicted values closely resembles that of the actual values. The 10th, 50th and 90th percentiles of the predicted distribution are 0.06, 1.09 and 6.9, respectively, compared to 0, 1 and 7 for the distribution of actual values.

4.4. Do People Cross State Borders to Get Payday Loans?

One key assumption for estimating equation (2) is that people who live near a state that allows payday lending actually travel across borders to get a payday loans. As Melzer (2011) discusses, considerable anecdotal evidence suggests traveling across the border to access payday lenders is fairly commonplace.[17] In addition, Melzer (2011) provides empirical evidence of increased payday store concentration in ZIP codes of states that allow payday lending and border states that prohibiting payday lending. Table 3 shows results of a similar analysis using the ZCBP data, which covers all states rather than just the ten states for which Melzer compiled payday lender location data. I run negative binomial regressions similar to (3), but include dummy variables for whether the ZIP code is within 25 miles of a ZIP code in a payday prohibiting state, and a general border dummy variable:

$$E(PDstores_z) = \exp\left\{\begin{array}{l}\alpha_0 + \alpha_1 \ln(pop_z) + \alpha_2 \ln(estab_z) + \mathbf{x}_z'\boldsymbol{\beta} \\ + \delta(near\ prohibiting\ state_z) + \lambda(border_z) + \theta(rural_z)\end{array}\right\} \quad (5)$$

---

[17] Additionally, for example, at the time of writing this paper Pennsylvania lawmakers were considering a law to allow payday lending in the state motivated in part by reports that Pennsylvania residents were getting payday loans anyway by traveling to other states.

I also include both rural and urban ZIP codes (of payday-allowing states) in the regression sample since payday lenders might also increase their presence in rural ZIP codes on borders, and I include a rural indicator variable in the regression.

The first column of table 3 shows a 12 percent increase in the number of payday stores in ZIP codes within 25 miles of a ZIP code in a payday prohibiting state relative to other ZIP codes in the same state, but the estimate is not quite statistically significant at the 5 percent level. The second column regression employs a quadratic in distance to other states, rather than the border dummy variable. The point estimate now is slightly larger (almost 15 percent) and statistically significant. The final column presents an estimate using only ZIP codes that are near a state border (that's why the sample size drops significantly). This specification identifies δ more stringently; the estimate indicates that ZIP codes near prohibiting states have 18 percent more payday lending stores, on average, relative to other border ZIP codes in the same state that are near other payday-allowing states. Notably, this estimate is quite similar in magnitude to Melzer's, and provides supportive evidence for the notion that people cross borders to obtain payday loans.

5. Do Payday Loans Affect Financial Well-Being?

5.1. Consumer Credit Record Data and Outcome Measures

The credit record data used in this paper come from the Federal Reserve Bank of New York Consumer Credit Panel/Equifax (CCP), a nationally representative longitudinal database with detailed information at a quarterly frequency on consumer debt and loan performance derived from consumer credit records maintained by Equifax, one of that nation's three major credit bureaus.[18] The CCP can be used to compute both nationally representative estimates at the end of a given quarter as well as to track changes in debt use and loan performance for a given individual over time.[19]

The CCP includes each person's year of birth, and the ZIP and census tract codes of their mailing address each quarter. With these geographic codes, I am able to merge the ZIP-level predictions on payday lender concentration and census tract level socioeconomic characteristics

---

[18] Lee and van der Klaaw (2010) provide a detailed discussion of these data.

[19] All individuals in the database are anonymous: names, street addresses and social security numbers have been suppressed. Individuals are distinguished and can be linked over time through a unique, anonymous consumer identification number assigned by Equifax.

from the 2000 Census to use as controls (in lieu of individual demographic data beyond age). Finally, in addition to detailed credit account information, the CCP also provides a credit score for most individuals, updated each quarter.[20] The Equifax credit score, like other credit scores, essentially summarizes the information in one's credit report and is based on a model that predicts the likelihood of becoming 90 days or more delinquent over the next 24 months. Credit scoring models include numerous factors such as the frequency and degree of delinquent accounts, the amount of credit being utilized, and recent applications for credit. Factors that are *not* considered include income and employment history as such information is not available in credit reports. The credit score ranges from 280-850, with a higher score corresponding to lower relative risk.

I drew three independent cross-sections of the data for 2007, 2009 and 2012, and in each cross section individuals are observed at both the beginning and end of the year.[21] Table 4 provides summary statistics for the four outcomes examined in the regressions: credit score at the end of the year, the probability of a score drop of 25 points or more over the course of the year, the probability of a new delinquency, and the probability of hitting one's credit limit on credit cards (general purpose and retail cards) conditional on utilizing less than 75 percent at the start of the year.[22] Panel A shows statistics for the full sample of consumers. The average credit score is almost 700, while the probability of experiencing a score decline of 25 percent or more is nearly 17 percent. The likelihood of a new delinquency is about 9 percent.[23] Finally, the probability of reaching or exceeding one's credit card limit is just 2.4 percent.

Panel B restricts the sample to those living in "payday ZIPs" (see Section 4.3). This restriction cuts the sample roughly in half, but the credit record statics are quite similar to the full sample. In other words, people living in the urban areas where payday lenders most likely to be highly concentrated are, on average, quite similar to the broad population in terms of their credit

---

[20] Some individuals at a point in time are not "scoreable" because of a limited credit history. The Equifax credit score is similar to the well-known FICO risk score. For more details, see https://help.equifax.com/app/answers/detail/a_id/244/related/1.

[21] I start with 2007 as opposed to 2006 because it comes after the FDIC guidance on the "rent-a-bank" model. Each cross section is an independent 25 percent of the full CCP.

[22] FICO considers score changes of less than 20 points as indicative of stability. See for instance http://bankinganalyticsblog.fico.com/2010/07/how-much-do-fico-scores-change-over-time.html.

[23] The CCP does not have account level information, but rather provides information on all accounts rolled up to the credit category level for ten different types of credit (e.g. credit cards, auto loans, etc.), such as the number of open accounts and the number of accounts in good standing. I identify individuals with a new delinquency as those who have at least one non-current account at the end of the year in a credit category in which they had at least one open account in that category at beginning of the year with all open accounts in the category in good standing.

record characteristics. Finally, Panel C restricts the sample further to borrowers likely to have high demand for payday loans. Based on information from BST (2012), the sample includes relatively young borrowers age 25-49, with no more than a $5,000 cumulative credit limit on credit cards at the start of the year, and who inquired about credit at least twice in the prior year.[24] Notably, the sample size drops by almost 90 percent, which seems appropriate given estimates that only about 5-10 percent of the population uses payday loans in a given year. This group has considerably lower credit scores than the general population, and are more likely to experience a score drop in excess of 25 points. The probability of a new delinquency is more than double what it is for the general population, and the probability of maxing out their credit card lines is substantially higher too. The regressions will test whether access to payday loans improves or worsens these outcomes.

Table 5 shows the distribution of ZIP codes and payday ZIPs across payday allowing and prohibiting states over time in 2007, 2009 and 2012. Between 2007 and 2009, about 800 ZIP codes move from the allowed group to the prohibited group, an increase of about 20 percent. As noted earlier, I define payday ZIPs as ZIP codes with a predicted payday lender concentration in the top one-third of all ZIP codes. Thus, of the 13,613 ZIP codes initially in the sample, one-third or 4,535 are payday ZIPs, and in 2007, 3,408 of these ZIPs were in payday allowing states and 1,127 were in payday prohibiting states.[25] By 2012, the number of payday ZIPs in prohibiting states increased by about 24 percent to 1,399.

The last row of table 5 shows the number of payday ZIPs in prohibiting states within 25 miles of a payday allowing state. There were 250 such ZIP codes in 2007, rising to just 272 by 2012. The steadiness of this number masks the fact that some ZIP codes fall out of this group over time (for example ZIP codes in Massachusetts near the border with New Hampshire lost access in 2009 when New Hampshire implemented a ban), and others enter (for example border ZIP codes in Arkansas that maintained access to payday loans through Tennessee despite the state's ban).

---

[24] Credit inquiries refer to specific instances when a lender requests a credit report for an individual because that individual was seeking a new credit account. Inquiries do not include instances when lenders pull credit reports without an individual's consent in order to conduct targeted marketing campaigns or for routine risk management procedures. Inquiries also do not include instances when a consumer requests his or her own credit report for monitoring purposes.

[25] Since the District of Columbia (DC) allowed payday loans for most of 2007, DC is considered an allowing state for 2007.

5.2. The Effect of Payday Loans on Credit Scores

Table 6 presents estimates of the effect of payday loans on credit scores and the probability of a score drop of at least 25 points. The first three columns show results for the level of credit scores using an unrestricted sample of consumers. In addition to the specifications discussed earlier with state fixed effects and state-by-year fixed effects, the first column shows estimates only with region-by-year fixed effects, thus allowing cross-state variation to help identify the effect of payday loans. The point estimate on the access variable in this regression implies that access to payday loans leads to a reduction in credit scores of just -2.86 points (note that the unemployment shock variable has been re-centered to have mean zero so that the coefficient on the access to payday loans variable is roughly equivalent to what it would be in a regression excluding the interaction term). The second column reports the results from estimating equation (1), which one might find more persuasive as it includes state fixed effects, but the result is little changed. The point estimate in this specification is only -1.14 points with a standard error, clustered at the state level, of 1.37 points. Finally, the third column reports results from estimating equation (2), which mirrors Melzer's (2011) identification strategy by including state-by-year fixed effects. Again, the point estimate is close to zero and insignificant.

The second row indicates that unemployment shocks have a statistically significant, but small, negative effect on credit scores in places that prohibit payday loans. As noted earlier, the unemployment shock variable is defined as the average unemployment rate in either 2007, 2009 or 2012 minus the average unemployment rate from 2000-2006; it has a standard deviation of about 2.5 percentage points. The small effect of this variable probably stems from county-level unemployment providing a rather noisy measure of individual unemployment. The coefficient on the interaction with payday loan access is also close to zero and insignificant. Thus, overall the regression results so far provide no evidence that payday loans affect credit scores.

As discussed in Section 3.2, one reason why the estimated effect over the unrestricted sample might be so close to zero is that the probability of using payday loans among the broad population is small. The next 3 columns show results for the same three specifications but using only the restricted sample of individuals, described in the previous section, most likely to have high demand for payday loans. The results over the narrow sample change sign (the effect of payday loans is now positive), but the point estimates remain close to zero. The largest estimate is in the middle column and is statistically significant, but the magnitude is only 2.8 points and the 95 percent confidence interval rules out effects in excess of 5.3 points.

The second half of table 6 presents estimates of the effect of payday loans on the probability of a score drop of 25 points or more over the course of the year. Focusing on the last two columns where the restricted sample is used and state and state-year fixed effects are included, respectively, the point estimates are negative (implying payday loans are beneficial) but close to zero and insignificant.

The sign on the interaction term in the last two regressions indicates that payday loans are more beneficial in places hit hard by labor market shocks, but the magnitude of the estimates are fairly small, which again may reflect the weakness of the correlation between county level unemployment and individual unemployment. With more precise data on individual employment status, it seems possible that the interaction effect could be economically important, but such data unfortunately are not available.[26]

5.3. Other Outcomes

Table 7 provides estimates the effect of payday loans on the likelihood of a new delinquency, and the likelihood of reaching or exceeding one's credit card limit. These two variables are closely connected to variables that play an important role in determining one's credit score.

The first two columns of table 7 show the preferred specifications with state and state-year fixed effects, respectively, over the restricted sample, and indicate a negative effect of payday loans on the likelihood of delinquency (that is, payday loans tend to be helpful in avoiding delinquency on traditional accounts), but the point estimates are small and statistically insignificant. Labor market shocks appear to have a significant effect on the likelihood of delinquency – a one standard deviation increase in the size of a county unemployment shock leads to about a two percentage point increase in the likelihood of a new delinquency. The sign on the interaction term is negative, suggesting that access to payday loans helps mitigate the negative effect of a labor market shock, but the estimate is not statistically significant.

---

[26] In contrast, Carrell and Zinman (2013) provide some evidence that high local unemployment exacerbates the negative effect of payday loans on military personnel performance. Although military personnel are, of course, employed, high unemployment could affect the employment status of a spouse and overall household income.

The last two columns of table 7 provide estimates of the effect of payday loans on the likelihood of hitting one's credit card limit. Again the point estimates are fairly small and statistically indistinguishable from zero.

5.4. Alternative Samples and Specifications

Table 8 provides alternative estimates of the effect of payday loans based on additional restrictions to the high payday loan demand subsample, as well as additional specifications where initial credit score is included as a control. The first two columns show estimates of the coefficient on the access variable in equations (1) and (2) using the restricted sample, but with the additional restriction of excluding those with initial credit scores in excess of 600. Panel A shows estimates for the effect of payday loans on credit scores at the end of the year. Though both point estimates are statistically significant, they are slightly smaller than in table 6 (fifth and sixth columns). As shown in the next two columns, after controlling for initial credit score, the coefficient is more precisely estimated but even smaller in magnitude at less than 1.5 points.

The next four columns provide estimates where the high demand subsample has a different additional restriction, limiting the sample to those with at least four inquiries in the past year instead of two. The first two estimates are again statistically significant, but small, and are not robust to controlling for initial credit score as seen in the last two columns.

Panels B, C and D provide estimates for the other three outcome variables. In general, the estimates point in the direction of payday loans being beneficial, but the magnitudes are small and insignificant. Perhaps a slight exception is that payday loans appear to reduce the likelihood of a 25 point score drop by about 1 percentage point, on average, for the low initial credit score subsample, but that is relative to a mean likelihood for this subsample of about 24 percent.

6. Discussion

Unlike previous research that finds both substantive positive and negative effects of payday loans on financial well-being, the empirical results in this paper suggest little connection (slightly beneficial, if anything). Differences in identification strategies could play some role in generating different results. For example, Skiba and Tobacman (2011) use data from a payday lender on a large set of applicants, exploit a discontinuity in the approval process, and find that payday loans increase the likelihood of (chapter 13) bankruptcy. But, as they point out, the estimated effect pertains to individuals near the discontinuity (in this case, those nearly rejected for a payday loan) and may have limited external validity. Morse (2011) also studies a particular situation, finding that access to payday loans mitigates the effect of natural disasters on foreclosures. These results may reflect the beneficial effects of access for a group that does not typically use payday loans. In contrast, the estimates in this paper may better reflect the effect of payday loans on credit record outcomes among the average credit constrained individual.

One advantage of using credit scores is that they are sensitive to all types of credit record events, including events less severe than bankruptcy or foreclosure. Thus, finding a null effect is meaningful, and suggests that payday loans, on average, are financially neither destabilizing nor greatly beneficial relative to a world without payday loans. On the one hand, this could be because alternatives to payday loans yield roughly similar positive or negative outcomes. For example, in the absence of payday loans consumers may instead bounce checks, as Zinman (2010) and Morgan et al (2012) find, which might be similarly destabilizing. On the other hand, it could be that payday loans are neither destabilizing nor greatly beneficial (in absolute terms) simply because they are small and unsecured, which limits both their benefits and risks.

One of the main empirical specifications adopts the identification strategy of Melzer (2011), who finds that households with access to payday loans report having substantially greater difficulty paying their mortgage, rent or other bills relative to similar households without access. Perhaps one way to reconcile the null results in this paper with Melzer's results is that the self-reported outcomes he studies may be picking up psychological strain associated with paying off a costly payday loan, but such stress does not progress into actual derogatory items on credit records.[27] That said, I study a different time period and many more states where payday lending is prohibited; these differences could also play a role in generating different results.

7. Conclusion

Strong growth in the payday loan market since the late 1990s has spurred a debate about the risks and benefits of payday loans. Academic research on this question has been inconclusive. Given the potentially more active regulatory environment following the 2010

---

[27] Somewhat similarly, Carrell and Zinman (2013) provide evidence that payday loans might cause mental or financial stress for members of the military.

Dodd-Frank Act and establishment of the CFPB, additional research is needed to better understand the payday loan market and its effects on consumers' financial well-being.

In this paper, I draw on nationally representative panel data comprised of individual credit records, as well as Census data on the location of payday loan shops at the ZIP code level, to test whether payday loans affects consumers' financial health, using credit scores and score changes, as well as other credit record variables, as measures of financial health. In order to identify the effect of payday loans, I take advantage of geographic and temporal variation in access arising from differences in state lending laws. In addition to standard identification strategies based on state law variation, I also follow Melzer's (2011) novel strategy of exploiting within-state variation in access to payday loans due to differences in the proximity of ZIP codes in states that prohibit payday lending to states that allow payday lending.

Overall, I find little to no effect of access to payday loans on credit scores and other credit record outcomes. The results contrast with previous research that finds payday loans have large effects, including on events such as bankruptcy and foreclosure, but could reflect differences in the time period studied, outcomes analyzed, or empirical strategies that identify the effect of payday loans off of different marginal borrowers.

Citations

Avery, Robert B. and Katherine A. Samolyk. 2011. "Payday Loans versus Pawnshops: The Effects of Loan Fee Limits on Household Use." Federal Reserve System Research Conference, Arlington, Virginia.

Bertrand, Marianne and Adair Morse. 2011. "Information Disclosure, Cognitive Biases and Payday Borrowing." *Journal of Finance* 66(6) p.1865-1893.

Bhutta, Neil, Paige Marta Skiba and Jeremy Tobacman. 2012. "Payday Loan Choices and Consequences." Vanderbilt Law and Economics Research Paper 12-30.

Carrell, Scott E. and Jonathan Zinman. 2013. "In Harm's Way? Payday Loan Access and Military Personnel Performance." Working Paper.

Caskey, John P. 2005. "Fringe Banking and the Rise of Payday Lending." *Credit Markets for the Poor.* Ed. Patrick Bolton and Howard Rosenthal. New York City, NY: Russell Sage Foundation. 17-45.

———. 2010. "Payday Lending: New Research and the Big Question." Federal Reserve Bank of Philadelphia Working Paper No. 10-32.

Consumer Federation of America. 2001. "Payday Lenders Evade State Consumer Protections by 'Renting' Bank Charters." Jack Gillis and Jean Ann Fox.

Consumer Financial Protection Bureau. 2013. "Payday Loans and Deposit Advance Products: A White Paper of Initial Data Findings."

Elliehausen, Gregory, and Edward C. Lawrence. 2001. "Payday Advance Credit in America: An Analysis of Customer Demand." Monograph no. 35, Credit Research Center, Georgetown University.

Federal Reserve Board. 2007. "Report to the Congress on Credit Scoring and Its Effects on the Availability and Affordability of Credit."

Laibson, D. 1997. "Golden eggs and hyperbolic discounting." *Quarterly Journal of Economics* 112: 443-77.

Lee, Donghoon and Wilbert Van der Klaauw. 2010. "An Introduction to the FRBNY Consumer Credit Panel." Federal Reserve Bank of New York Staff Report No. 479.

Mann, Ronald J. and James Hawkins. 2007. "Just Until Payday." UCLA Law Review 54.

Melzer, Brian T. 2011. The Real Costs of Credit Access: Evidence from the Payday Lending Market. *The Quarterly Journal of Economics* Vol. 126, Issue 1 (February 2011): 517-55.

Morgan, Donald P. and Michael Strain. 2008. "Payday Holiday: How Households Fare After Payday Credit Bans." Federal Reserve Bank of New York Staff Report No. 309.

Morgan, Donald P., Michael Strain and Ihab Seblani. 2012. "How Payday Credit Access Affects Overdrafts and Other Outcomes." *Journal of Money, Credit and Banking* 44: 519-531.

Morse, Adair. 2011. "Payday lenders: Heroes or Villains?" *Journal of Financial Economics* Vol. 102, Issue 1: 28-44.

Prager, Robin A. 2009. "Determinants of the Locations of Payday Lenders, Pawnshops and Check-Cashing Outlets." Federal Reserve Board of Governors Finance and Economic Discussion Working paper 2009-33.

Skiba, Paige Marta and Jeremy Tobacman. 2011. "Do Payday Loans Cause Bankruptcy?"

———. 2008. "Payday Loans, Uncertainty, and Discounting: Explaining Patterns of Borrowing, Repayment, and Default." Vanderbilt University Law School Law and Economics Working Paper No. 08-33.

Stegman, Michael A. 2007. "Payday Lending." *The Journal of Economic Perspectives* Vol. 21, Number 1: 169-190(22).

Zinman, Jonathan. 2010. "Restricting consumer credit access: Household survey evidence on effects around the Oregon rate cap." *Journal of Banking & Finance* Vol. 34, Issue 3: 546-56.

Figure 1. State payday lending regulations over time

State	2006	2007	2008	2009	2010	2011	2012
Alabama	Legal	Legal	Legal	Legal	Legal	Legal	Legal
Alaska	Legal	Legal	Legal	Legal	Legal	Legal	Legal
Arizona	Legal	Legal	Legal	Legal	Legal→Prohibited	Prohibited	Prohibited
Arkansas	Legal	Legal	Legal→Prohibited	Prohibited	Prohibited	Prohibited	Prohibited
California	Legal	Legal	Legal	Legal	Legal	Legal	Legal
Colorado	Legal	Legal	Legal	Legal	Heavily restricted	Heavily restricted	Heavily restricted
Connecticut	Prohibited	Prohibited	Prohibited	Prohibited	Prohibited	Prohibited	Prohibited
Delaware	Legal	Legal	Legal	Legal	Legal	Legal	Legal
District of Columbia	Legal	Legal→Prohibited	Prohibited	Prohibited	Prohibited	Prohibited	Prohibited
Florida	Legal	Legal	Legal	Legal	Legal	Legal	Legal
Georgia	Prohibited	Prohibited	Prohibited	Prohibited	Prohibited	Prohibited	Prohibited
Hawaii	Legal	Legal	Legal	Legal	Legal	Legal	Legal
Idaho	Legal	Legal	Legal	Legal	Legal	Legal	Legal
Illinois	Legal	Legal	Legal	Legal	Legal	Legal	Legal
Indiana	Legal	Legal	Legal	Legal	Legal	Legal	Legal
Iowa	Legal	Legal	Legal	Legal	Legal	Legal	Legal
Kansas	Legal	Legal	Legal	Legal	Legal	Legal	Legal
Kentucky	Legal	Legal	Legal	Legal	Legal	Legal	Legal
Louisiana	Legal	Legal	Legal	Legal	Legal	Legal	Legal
Maine	Heavily restricted	Heavily restricted	Heavily restricted	Heavily restricted	Heavily restricted	Heavily restricted	Heavily restricted
Maryland	Prohibited	Prohibited	Prohibited	Prohibited	Prohibited	Prohibited	Prohibited
Massachusetts	Prohibited	Prohibited	Prohibited	Prohibited	Prohibited	Prohibited	Prohibited
Michigan	Legal	Legal	Legal	Legal	Legal	Legal	Legal
Minnesota	Legal	Legal	Legal	Legal	Legal	Legal	Legal
Mississippi	Legal	Legal	Legal	Legal	Legal	Legal	Legal
Missouri	Legal	Legal	Legal	Legal	Legal	Legal	Legal
Montana	Legal	Legal	Legal	Legal	Legal	Prohibited	Prohibited
Nebraska	Legal	Legal	Legal	Legal	Legal	Legal	Legal
Nevada	Legal	Legal	Legal	Legal	Legal	Legal	Legal
New Hampshire	Legal	Legal	Legal	Prohibited	Prohibited	Prohibited	Prohibited
New Jersey	Prohibited	Prohibited	Prohibited	Prohibited	Prohibited	Prohibited	Prohibited
New Mexico	Legal	Legal	Legal	Legal	Legal	Legal	Legal
New York	Prohibited	Prohibited	Prohibited	Prohibited	Prohibited	Prohibited	Prohibited
North Carolina	Prohibited	Prohibited	Prohibited	Prohibited	Prohibited	Prohibited	Prohibited
North Dakota	Legal	Legal	Legal	Legal	Legal	Legal	Legal
Ohio	Legal	Legal	Legal	Legal	Legal	Legal	Legal
Oklahoma	Legal	Legal	Legal	Legal	Legal	Legal	Legal
Oregon	Legal	Legal	Heavily restricted	Heavily restricted	Heavily restricted	Heavily restricted	Heavily restricted
Pennsylvania	Prohibited	Prohibited	Prohibited	Prohibited	Prohibited	Prohibited	Prohibited
Rhode Island	Lightly restricted	Lightly restricted	Lightly restricted	Lightly restricted	Lightly restricted	Lightly restricted	Lightly restricted
South Carolina	Legal	Legal	Legal	Legal	Legal	Legal	Legal
South Dakota	Legal	Legal	Legal	Legal	Legal	Legal	Legal
Tennessee	Legal	Legal	Legal	Legal	Legal	Legal	Legal
Texas	Legal	Legal	Legal	Legal	Legal	Legal	Legal
Utah	Legal	Legal	Legal	Legal	Legal	Legal	Legal
Vermont	Prohibited	Prohibited	Prohibited	Prohibited	Prohibited	Prohibited	Prohibited
Virginia	Legal	Legal	Legal	Legal	Legal	Legal	Legal
Washington	Legal	Legal	Legal	Legal	Legal	Legal	Legal
West Virginia	Prohibited	Prohibited	Prohibited	Prohibited	Prohibited	Prohibited	Prohibited
Wisconsin	Legal	Legal	Legal	Legal	Legal	Legal	Legal
Wyoming	Legal	Legal	Legal	Legal	Legal	Legal	Legal

Key: Legal, Lightly restricted, Prohibited, Heavily restricted

Note: See footnote 9 of text for list of information sources.

Figure 2. Concentration of payday lending establishments versus other credit industry establishments, by state legal status of payday loans in 2008

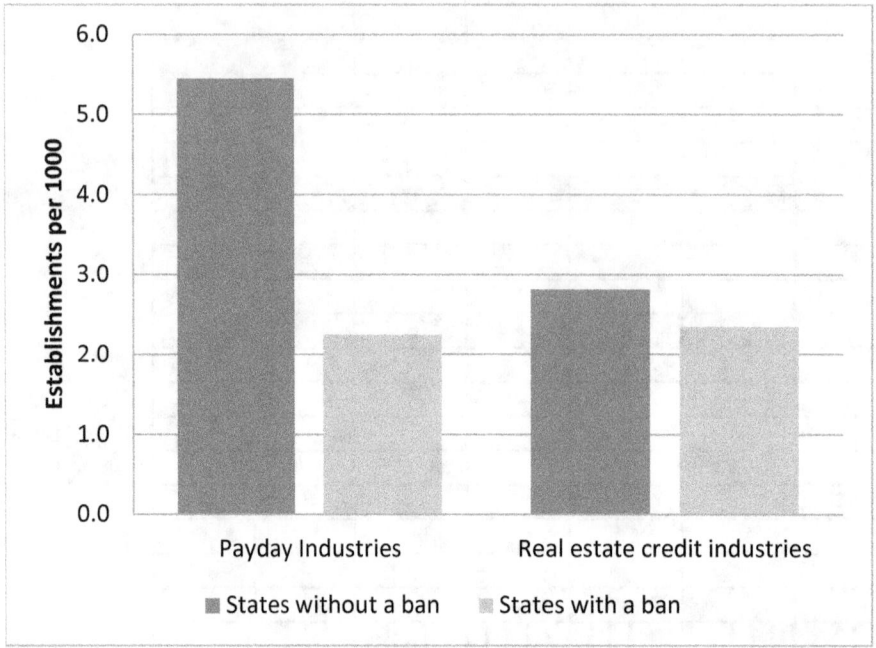

Source: Author's calculations from 2008 Census ZIP Code Business Patterns data

Figure 3: Concentration of payday loan industry establishments over time, by legal status

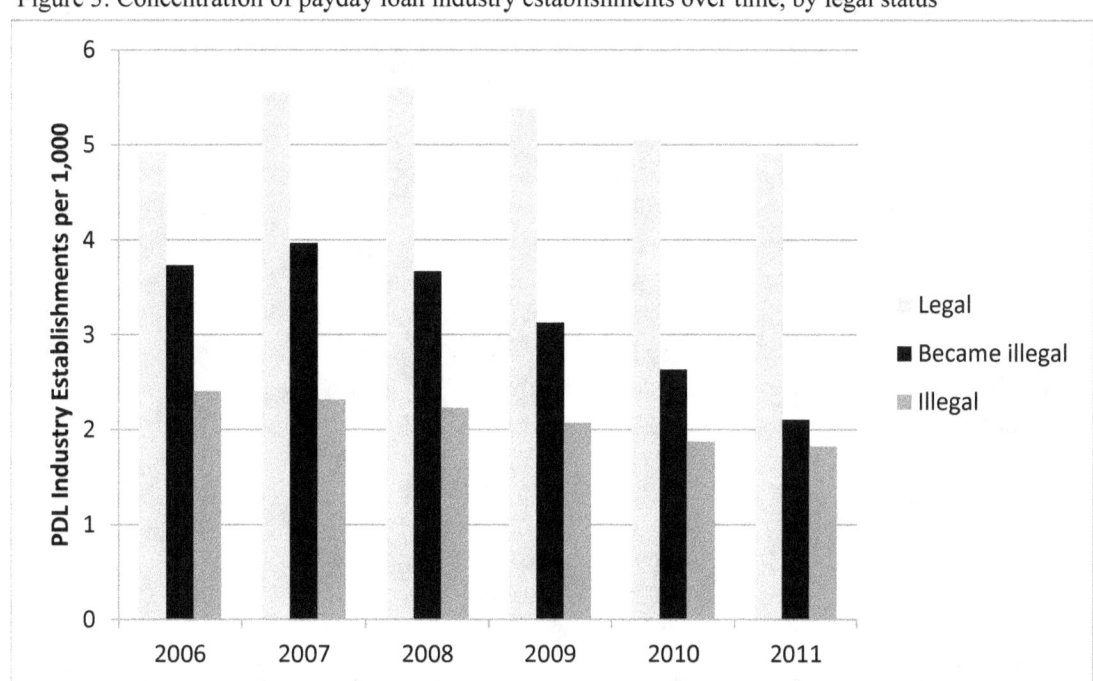

Notes: Author's calculations from Census Business Patterns data. See figure 1 for states that banned payday lending during this period

Table 1: Descriptive statistics for ZIP codes in states allowing payday lending from 2006-2012

	Mean	Std. Dev.	10th Percentile	50th Percentile	90th Percentile	N
ZIP Code Business Patterns data						
Number of payday establishments[1]	2.4	4.0	0	1	7	8666
Total number of establishments[2]	409	454	27	243	1028	8666
Annual payroll per employee ($, 000's)[3]	25	11	16	23	36	8666
Census 2000 ZIP code characteristics						
Population	17242	15718	1898	12786	39006	8666
Median family income	52362	19151	32303	49298	75206	8666
Median house value ($, 000s)	127	96	57	101	215	8663
Homeownership rate	0.71	0.18	0.47	0.76	0.89	8666
Prop 25+ years w/ at least a B.A.	0.22	0.15	0.08	0.18	0.44	8666
Share of adults under 40 years old	0.42	0.10	0.32	0.41	0.53	8666
Single-mother share of families	0.097	0.060	0.044	0.081	0.168	8666
Asian share of population	0.026	0.055	0.001	0.008	0.065	8666
Black share of population	0.10	0.18	0.002	0.026	0.32	8666
Hispanic share of population	0.11	0.18	0.007	0.030	0.33	8666

1. Number of establishments as of March 2008 in industries with NAICS code 522291 or 522390
2. As of 2000
3. As of 2000, calculated as aggregate ZIP code payroll divided by aggregate ZIP code number of employees for establishments in that ZIP code

Table 2a: ZIP-code-level negative binomial regression estimates of the relationship between the number of payday establishments and socio-economic characteristics

	outcome variable: # $PDstores_z$	
	(1)	(2)
ln(Population)	0.3752**	0.3540**
	(0.0361)	(0.0373)
ln(Total number of establishments)	1.0996**	1.1050**
	(0.0604)	(0.0626)
Median family income ($ 0,000's)	1.2151**	1.3417**
	(0.2814)	(0.2169)
(Median family income)^2	-0.2224**	-0.2387**
	(0.0525)	(0.0428)
(Median family income)^3	0.0175**	0.0184**
	(0.0041)	(0.0035)
(Median family income)^4	-0.0005**	-0.0005**
	(0.0001)	(0.0001)
ln(Annual payroll per employee)	-0.3639**	-0.3835**
	(0.0380)	(0.0362)
ln(Median home value)	-0.5155**	-0.5534**
	(0.0714)	(0.0720)
Owner-occupancy rate	-0.2914	-0.3015
	(0.2292)	(0.2383)
Prop 25+ years w/ at least a B.A.	-1.4976**	-1.4541**
	(0.2712)	(0.2705)
Share of adults under 40 years old	0.9469**	0.8077**
	(0.2251)	(0.2389)
Single-mother share of families	1.1592*	1.3026**
	(0.4881)	(0.4847)
Asian share of population		0.3600*
		(0.1629)
Black share of population		0.0891
		(0.1400)
Hispanic share of population		0.2816
		(0.1655)
Constant	-7.6807**	-7.5767**
	(0.5248)	(0.5366)
log-likelihood	-12154.14	-12148.22
N	8663	8663

Standard errors clustered at the state level. *p<0.05, **p<0.01. Both models include state-level fixed effects.

Table 2b: Estimated impact of a one standard deviation in explanatory variable on number of payday establishments, all else constant, based on estimated coefficients from Table 3a (column 2).

Explanatory variable	Impact
ln(Population)	48.5%
ln(Total number of establishments)	350.4%
Median family income[1]	20.6%
ln(Annual payroll per employee)	-12.2%
ln(Median home value)	-26.2%
Owner-occupancy rate	-5.2%
Prop 25+ years w/ at least a B.A.	-19.5%
Share of adults under 40 years old	8.0%
Single-mother share of families	8.2%
Asian share of population	2.0%
Black share of population	1.6%
Hispanic share of population	5.2%

1. Effect was calculated using a one standard deviation increase ($20,000) from $40,000 (25th percentile of *median family income*)

Table 3: Negative binomial estimates of the effect of being near a payday prohibiting state on the number of ZIP code payday lending establishments

	outcome variable: # *PDstoresz*		
	(1)	(2)	(3)
ZIP code within 25 miles of payday prohibiting state	0.1239 (0.0683)	0.1486* (0.0635)	0.1879* (0.0886)
ZIP code within 25 miles of another state	0.0352 (0.0375)		
Distance (in miles) to another state		-0.0003 (0.0008)	
Squared distance to another state		0.0000 (0.0000)	
ln(L)	-17,342	-17,342	-4,310
N	20,327	20,327	5,744

Notes: * $p < 0.05$; ** $p < 0.01$. Standard errors in parentheses clustered at the MSA level. Sample for the first two regressions are all ZIP codes in payday-allowing states; the third regression includes only those ZIP codes within 25 miles of a ZIP code in another state. All regressions include state fixed effects, an indicator for urban/rural status of the ZIP code, and the set of controls used for the regression shown in column 2 of table 2a.

4. Credit record data summary statistics

	Score[1]	25 point or more score drop	New delinquency[2]	Max out credit lines[3]
		A. Unrestricted sample		
Mean	699.4	0.166	0.089	0.024
Std dev	109.9	0.372	0.284	0.153
N	4,049,409	4,049,409	3,738,497	3,064,339
		B. Individuals living in payday ZIPs[4]		
Mean	690.6	0.169	0.094	0.026
Std dev	111.8	0.375	0.292	0.160
N	1,920,433	1,920,433	1,750,514	1,404,244
		C. Individuals likely to have high PDL demand[5]		
Mean	573.7	0.249	0.230	0.107
Std dev	91.9	0.433	0.421	0.309
N	216,175	216,175	170,636	81,067

Notes: Statistics for pooled 2007, 2009 and 2012 cross sections from the FRBNY CCP/Equifax; in each cross section, individuals are observed at both the beginning and end of year.
1. Equifax risk score measured at end of year
2. Was 30 days or more late on at least one account by the end of the year in at least one credit category, with at least one open account in that category at the beginning of the year and all accounts in that category current at the beginning of the year.
3. Borrowers who reach or exceed credit limit on either general purpose credit cards or retail store cards by the end of year, conditional on utilizing no more than 75 percent of their limits at the beginning of the year
4. "Payday ZIPs" refer to ZIP codes with a high predicted concentration of payday lenders (see text in Section 3 for more)
5. Consumers living in payday ZIPs age 25-49, with no more than $5,000 cumulative credit limit on credit cards at the start of the year, and had at least 2 inquiries in the prior year; traits chosen based on findings from Bhutta, Skiba and Tobacman (2012).

Table 5: Number of ZIP codes in payday allowing and prohibiting states

	2007		2009		2012	
	PDL Allowed	PDL Prohibited	PDL Allowed	PDL Prohibited	PDL Allowed	PDL Prohibited
Number of ZIP codes meeting initial sample selection criteria*	9,467	4,146	9,092	4,521	8,666	4,947
"Payday ZIPs" **	3,408	1,127	3,292	1,243	3,136	1,399
Share	36%	27%	36%	27%	36%	28%
"Payday ZIPs" within 25 miles of a payday-allowing state	n/a	250	n/a	270	n/a	272

*See Section 4.1 of text for description of sample selection criteria
** See Section 3.3 of text for description of how payday ZIPs are predicted

www.ingramcontent.com/pod-product-compliance
Lightning Source LLC
Chambersburg PA
CBHW081812170526
45167CB00008B/3415